JESUS IS MY PEN, GOD IS MY PAPER

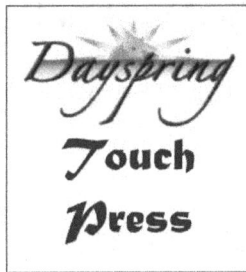

Dayspring
Touch
Press

By Lily Thompson

Jesus Is My Pen, God Is My Paper
Written by
Lily Thompson

ISBN 9780692587096

Library of Congress

Dayspring Touch Press
2127 Doctor's Park Drive
Columbus, IN 47203

Dedication

I would like to dedicate this book to a power greater than myself, from whom all of my blessings flow. I also dedicate it to my late mother and father Dorothy Thompson and William Thompson Sr. for all of their loving kindness. As well as all the people that believed in me throughout the years.

Special Thanks and

Acknowledgments

I would like to give thanks to the faculty of the Rockville and Madison Corrections facility for women. Thank you all for helping my life become relived and relearned. Thank you for all your time and encouragement. I would also like to thank all the inmates, for sharing their lives with me. I wish you all the best.

Special thanks, to Barbara and Tony Fulton, for welcoming me into your loving family. Special thanks also to my, sons Deon Thompson and William Thompson III, for never giving up on me.

Foreword

Use me Lord in your service. Anoint me to do your will in your way. My solemn prayer each and every day is to be of service to the Lord. **"But now, O Lord, thou art our father; we are the clay and thou our potter; and we all are the work of thy hand." (Isaiah 64:8).** This reminds us to always deny ourselves and follow His way in the Spirit of His will.

"My heart is inditing a good matter; I speak of the things which I have made touching the king: my tongue is the pen of a ready writer." (Psalms 45:1). "Jesus Is My Pen, God Is My Paper", is a book of poems to cause us to reflect, appreciate and experience the joy of the Lord. The "Significance of Man" and "Guarded", are just examples of the Lord being able to show our purpose and gives us the confidence to know the God is "Still in Control".

In this book, you are sure to find, words of encouragement in times of need. Always, mindful that we are vessels which the Lord wishes to use in His service. We are but the clay being molded by the "Great Potter".

Enjoy the verses, poems and inner thoughts. Reflect on the goodness of our Lord and Savior who awaits our obedience to be the "Ready Writer", the voice crying His

5

greatness, and giving honor to Him always. I trust Kingdom Building is in you. This book will provide you with the encouragement to seek the Lord at all times and to give praise to our Heavenly Father who sits on high looking low. All while we are awaiting His return to bring His saints unto Himself.

God bless you as you continue your journey and relationship with our Lord and Savior, Jesus Christ.

Pastor Steven L. Millon
God's House Missionary Baptist Church

JESUS IS MY PEN

Contents

Jesus Is My Pen, God Is My Paper   1

JESUS IS MY PEN

Introduction

Jesus Is My Pen, God Is My Paper

I write and write, it comes so plain. I write my words in Jesus name. All the things that come to mind, comes to me in Jesus time, just when or where things go, I do not know. I made a vow on bending knees, for with my life Jesus please, lead me guide me, with faithful hand. I will do what is Jesus' plan, my life no longer belong to me, for I love the things Jesus helps me see. So many faces and so much time, I'm glad to know that Jesus is mine, to teach me, direct me that's what Jesus will do, so I will always follow through. I talk to Jesus all the time, sometimes out loud, sometimes in my mind. Jesus is never too busy or makes a fuss, in Jesus alone, is where I put my trust.

Lily Thompson

JESUS IS MY PEN

Chapter 1

The Church

In the presence of God, just take a seat. Jesus is real, my heart repeats. The pews are long and the air is alive you can feel Jesus, as you come inside. So many faces the atmosphere is great everyone gets seated we can hardly wait. The music starts playing the choir is there, the sound of their voices fills the air. The hands are clapping joyous feelings inside, we sang to the heaven "YES JESUS IS ALIVE".

The music ends with the last note, the pastor calls our attention by clearing his throat. The first word he speaks starts a commotion "HALLELUJAH, HALLELUJAH", now we all got the notion, "HALLELUJAH, HALLELUJAH" we say from the pews, we settle once again as he looks at his shoes. He seems to be studying on the word that he hears and in an instant he shouts "JESUS IS HERE". The silence fills the room, as our savior appears he is right there in your heart, I could feel him right here. He assures me he loves me, tells me don't make a sound. My eyes fling open as I take a look

12

around, everyone in the building knows him for themselves, the experience is so holy I, love how it feels. My eyes close, I relax once again, the comforting spirit says "I am your friend". The air is alive, this is true. Just know in your heart that Jesus lives in you.

The Significance Of A Man

Let's put in words, before man there was chirping of
birds, before man there were skies and seas.
The earth had all things before the bending of knees.

The significance of man is not how he looks, it doesn't
matter if he has hands or hooks.

The significance of a man is not what he might say,
because one day his voice will fade away.

The significance of a man may cause you to assume, like
what really matters is how close is the moon, or that we
all wonder what will happen to things?

The significance of a man is believing in him, no not man
himself as we often do.
Pitying ourselves as we go through.

Life is a gift given to the world, who birthed life that's
what man should tell.

So,
The significance of a man is not being strong, it should be
seeking the almighty throne.
It should be of knowledge of his precious gifts, with his
words not speaking of myths.
The significance of a man is the truth that will save, save
us from death and the hurt of the ice cold grave,

14

it should be wisdom to talk to the king, knowing without God we could do nothing.

It should be to teach the world for that which we stand, it should be of the ruler of the land.

The significance of a man should be to continue to pray, it should be to gather God's children to hear what God has to say.

We long for knowledge to do many things, passion for possessions ruling everything.

The significance of a man should be on God's side, to take dominion over earth, knowing why Jesus died.

To use God's power and his strength, to defeat Satan himself.
It shouldn't be who has what or all the wealth.

The significance of a man should live in God's word, teaching all the world assuring that everyone has heard,

To spread God's goodness and all of God's praise, until Christ returns to this earth one day.

I Believe In Angels

Angels here angels there, in fact there's angels everywhere. No matter where you look you'll see one there. Don't look too hard for there not far. One could be riding in your car, they could be at your dinner table, you should know that you are able, to spot an angel anywhere you go. They are the ones that show loving kindness and a pleasant smile, they are patient and they show they care, they let you know they will always be there. So look around and you will an angel called you and me.

Carefully Taught

What has my life consisted of? What can I say, I have been playing around with substances that messed up my days. I've been blinded by the ignorance that clouded all my good thoughts. I refused to the things that I was so carefully taught. I choose to live my life as simple as it seemed, in worldly things and hatred for the living king. I tried so hard to change, to change those things that I could not change. I was sure I had the wisdom, so much I can-not explain, I followed excitement that turned into so much pain and lose. I asked for a miracle, my life I had to toss. I have been giving an example of the life I live today. I cannot promise you tomorrow, but I have seen this in such an awesome way. The hope that was given the grace that we do share, has changed my life and now I am so aware. Of the God that changed me in an instant, I choose to walk with thee my soul is very happy because Jesus first loved me. Jesus shows his strength and power, for no one saves them self. Jesus removed my doubts, of living to please everyone else. The question has been asked, your life is not your own, just give your life to Jesus and he will lead you on.

JESUS IS MY PEN

Chapter 2

I Don't Want To Miss It

The reason we have life, how do we choose our husband or how will be our wife? What will tomorrow bring? How will I get started or will I even try? Will I live or will I die? To focus on the finer things that's what most would say but what about the fact that these things will fade away? Dreamers have a better chance that is what some believe. Nothing comes to dreamers but night mares and more dreams. How about all the discoveries to give us all some clues? How about all the things that we see on the news? Take a look at the past if we are to understand at all. Things will come up and so many things will fall. We search for the wonders that are yet in this world. We look at all the faces of every boy or girl. Mystery after mystery the question still remains, how did this all get started? The answer stays the same. God our creator, Jesus as his only begotten son, died just to save us. For this race we all will run, glory to the father he forgives us one and all. Jesus left his holy spirit the comforter of this world. The brightness of the sun will blind us, you know is the solid truth. We all need a savior through the struggles we will face. These things keep us together to see God's amazing grace. I don't want to miss it not a single thing, I know the world wants to witness

Jesus return again

Guarded

Fenced, the fullness releasing my thoughts, all of life's lessons completing my walk. Guarded, by the sounds that no one has heard before. Singing of God's goodness, colored by the birds. Sunlight, yet moonlight the sparkles of the stars, chased by the clouds from near yet far. Rivers and oceans, puddles and streams, rain cease reflections are seen. Holding all boundaries, knowing all things, God's unchanging presence will always remain.

Transform Life

I, have met so many people, my life I've seen through theirs. God has given me wisdom, he has made me aware. I have been called to testify, the life I that I have lived through. To help the ones before me, to see themselves as loved. To challenge the way of change, to become what God created, to pray in Jesus name. To open to God's word of knowledge, to teach us the way. To put our trust in Jesus, his life he lived to die. To depend on the strength of Jesus, by given us a new life. To see our lives as blessings that we are called to be used. To give the glory to Christ Jesus, agree that this is the life we choose. To testify God's goodness, to spread the good news. To allow the ones we meet to be loved like Jesus do. Sharing the words in scripture, to know the living Christ. To challenge the way of change.

To transform someone's life.

Sight

Now, I see through the glass...<u>darkly</u>.

Now, I see through the darken glass. I see my future, I

see my past. <u>Vaguely</u>

Moving, at a study paste, I can see Jesus face to face.

<u>Slightly</u>

A glow that lights the darken room. I am sure of safety, I

am sure of doom. <u>Partly</u>

The suffering of your neighbors near. The starving

children can you hear? <u>Softly</u>

The thoughts that cross your mind, what will I do? Will I

have time? <u>Somehow</u>

A glimpse of what tomorrow brings, Will I dance or will

I sing? <u>Nicely</u>

The glass where the darkness dwell, am I cursed? Put

under a spell? The truth is clear soon will appear my

savior. <u>Quickly</u>

Now, I see the light so brightly with no shadow, it

follows the night. <u>Always</u>

I Made It Home

I, woke this morning and I thought of her, the love of my life. My loving mother her smile so alive. One kiss on the cheek, saying "dear child don't you weep". Remember the stories I told you before, I've done all I could to teach you right. Now, I am at rest so you can sleep at night. We will be together, just continue to pray. I, had to go with the savior, so you could know the way. You may miss me, I wish I could be there. Do not let your heart be troubled, have no despair. Peace at last, even though I am gone. One thing for sure,

I have made it home.

JESUS IS MY PEN

Chapter 3

In Jesus Hand

In this place where I stand alone, my mind often wonders to a place called home. God's word in which, I often seek. God tells me of that one so meek, precious as a new born child. The sound of peace will last for miles, the sun that shines so bright at noon. The streams and meadows everything in tune. The love we share as human beings, as we laugh and run through meadows and streams. The sun that shine so bright at noon, somehow ends too soon. No place that I could ever be, would be so lonesome, without Jesus with me. I search my heart, and to be so meek, the softened words I somehow speak. The previous love that we long, knowing that we are almost home. Wherever the place you may stand, keep your hand in Jesus hand.

Being A Christian

When it is hard to be a Christian, when you can't hold your tongue. When you don't want to help, instead you would rather run. When you are lonely inside and you need so much help. When you are only human, what should you do? Sometimes it is hard to be a Christian, when you are surrounded by deceit. Where no one is remorseful, when no one ever weeps. When no one cares how you really feel, not knowing all you want to do is God's will. When your nights short and your days are long, and all you want to do is go home. Where your friends aren't so friendly and things are too hard to bare. When everyone is talking and that is all you can hear, your mind seems to drift and you are no longer there. When struggles are plenty and you try not to complain. When it is hard to be a Christian, because no one understands. After the struggle and your thoughts get you nowhere. You may even have an outburst and still no one cares. You do all the things that seem loving and kind, when there is only one things going through others minds. You would hope that you could show them with wisdom and grace. You have spoken to Jesus and seeking his face. You have prayed for their loved ones as well as themselves. You have asked God for patience and guidance in loosing yourself. You find yourself hurting angry and upset. Jesus says to you in that gentle voice, "child believe in me, don't ever doubt, their time will come to know how you feel, and all they will want to do is my holy will. They will feel all the things that you feel tonight, you just keep doing the things that you know is right, when I made my promises it went out to all. This road may be long, but one day you will see. Fall on your face, for I know the way." Jesus will help you hear the words that a Christian should say. Jesus hears all your prayers lifted up in his name. When you have done all that you can do, don't worry about the things you can't fix yourself. When being a Christian seems that it may not work, know you have been chosen so never give up. Things are changing, things you may not see. Being a Christian is what we were born to be.

Nothing Left

As life brings its many twist, the thirst of air, that sudden quench. The words spoken so long they last, that only what you do for Christ will last. The words that were spoken from God himself, the words that speak of everlasting and wealth. The chance of peace and soul salvation. As life brings its twist, the turn has been taken. The words of wisdom will surely come, words were spoken taken life as a bless it token. Spending time in worship, the word was spoken giving life to creation. With every life formed placed in its own nation. The bird the trees yes every creation. The moon the stars with a single breath, leaving nothing no nothing left. The twist of leisurely turning, everything in life surely yearning. The blessing it gives of love and salvation, the twist of life is always enhancing. The words that was spoken from God himself leaves nothing, no nothing left.

When The Pains Of Death Surrounds Me

For Jesus delivers my soul, I am alive and once again whole. I am grateful to the Lord, who saved me, from this world and beyond. I am so glad that he forgives me, for all the things that I have done wrong. When the pain of death surrounds me on his strength I do depend, for it is so hard when you lose your next of kin. I thank the God that gave me her love, I will always have the sound of her laughter. I will have the moments when she became angry, the benefits of her presents has made me more aware. When she is no longer with me, Jesus will always be there. I am thankful for the time he gave us, the lessons that I have learned. When the pains of death surround me, Lord protect my heart and mind. Lord, give me the faith and wisdom to do what I have been told. To give my life to Jesus and to know that I have been saved by his blood. Lord allow me to give you the praise that you so gratefully deserve. Do not let my mind be troubled, for when the pain is so savior. I truly

31

miss her and wish she was still here,   Lord I am your grateful servant my life I give to you. I hear her words of wisdom and know just what to do, pay vows to the Lord of mercy, ruler of life and death, give praises to the Lord Jesus who knows that I have been truly blessed.

God's Will

God's plan for my life was quite different from what I wanted it to be. As I look around, I'm just where I should be. Through my life of troubles so much I misunderstood. The road that I had traveled in darkness, I thought I would never get out of the woods. Then something struck me, it was like a flash of light, everything inside me wanted to change that night. I really did not know, I could not understand, that is when I heard Jesus saying "Lily take my hand". I thought I was just dreaming, I was scared to death, but then there came the question "what do you really have left?" All odds were now against me, but still no pressure did I feel. I heard that familiar whisper saying "All things will be well." My heart filled with gladness, my eyes filled with tears. I had to ask the question "Is that why I have been given all these years?" Silence filled my being, stillness filled the air and for once in my life I felt the presence of Jesus there. In a jail cell cold and dirty, with nothing much to eat I looked for his face, but I could only see his

33

feet. The heavens wrapped around me, I heard "You will never be alone, God's awesome blessing is to make heaven your home". I heard Jesus' calming whisper, it said "Follow me my child, 18 years may seem strict, but I will be with you all the while. I have to mold you into the person that you were born to be. If you choose my wisdom you will surely see. This life I sit before you now take a closer look. I have a plan for you as you begin to write my book. It will help the ones that need it and those that are unsure. The book that you are writing is my windows and my doors." Yes it happened to me and on this very day, these words that God placed in me, I will write till my dying day. Yes, there was a struggle but soon it will become plain. I am the one chosen so I write in Jesus' name.

JESUS IS MY PEN

Chapter 4

Faith

Faith is a mountain you climb with all your might, sure it may scare you considering the heights. You have to struggle, for the struggle is steep that is when you pray admitting that you are weak. The adventure is the greatest, it is the best of all sometimes you may slip other times you might fall. The mountain is sturdy, it will hold all your weight every step you take you can hardly wait. So much going on around you, so you must concentrate keeping your mind on Jesus, for his strength is what it takes. You may get hungry, and sleepy sometimes you will bleed. You know in your heart that the climb is quite needed, the wind will be whispering "keep going don't you dare stop", this whisper will help you get to the top. Your harness is Jesus, he will hold you in place. You will begin to look for more than this human rat race, your body will tremble, the climb may seem to be too hard. Jesus, says try him, so where will you start? At the bottom of the mountain, where the ground is very close your mind may become weary, but you do not have another choice. When you look at the mountain, faith is your friend, and Jesus will be with you holding your hand. Your climb to the top, becomes just what you seek. Once you start climbing grace will place your feet on every stone that holds you, to the peak you will know you are getting closer and to heaven you will go. Faith is a mountain you climb for your life, you might be scared considering the heights. Prayer is the answer, to renew you from all doubt. Jesus is the love you cannot live without.

Life Is An Instrument

Can you hear the sound it is moving through the air? It beats through the ground, practice the tempo the volume is just right. Your instruction is prayer. The scale is faith, not sight. Watch as you listen, the elements everywhere, clapping to rhythm. Surely, Jesus is right there. Singing to the father who mounts on high. The symphony of glory don't let it pass you by.

On God You Can Depend

To solve all life's problems, for what may seem so bad. Just look for Jesus in everything you have. Never be doubtful, because test will come. The promise is given to all not just a few, when you read your bible you will know Jesus is talking to you. I am all you will ever need and now that you know, you must take me with you wherever you go. No weapon has been formed, to defeat God himself, so why would you depend on anyone else? The more you read your bible you will find that it is true, the ones that you have tried to help you. Your mother, your sisters even your best friends. Only on God you can depend.

Jesus Is A Friend Of Mine

My mother called to me with tears in her eyes, she said "the words I am about to say, I hope one day you realize. Sit down my dear, then she took my hand. What I am about to say I pray you understand, she looked so deep into my eyes, at that moment she begin to say. Jesus, wants to be your friend, someday you will see." Trouble seemed to have its hold, in prison I did land, my mind became so confused, I had so much to say. The day I heard God's gentle voice, it pierced my heart and soul, saying "You my child belong to me no matter just how old." That is the moment my life hit me it was like a flash of light, at that instant I realized all my life Jesus has been a friend of mine.

The Bible

Why do I read the Bible? For the stories do unfold, it answers many questions that I've always wanted to know.   The truth reveal the power, of the spirit left behind. The reading stays in my memory, it stays with me all the time. I am happy that it was written, the events that did take place. I am happy to learn the customs of the ancient human race. I am happy to know the seasons, behind the do's and don'ts.   With the knowledge that I have been given, for the reasons for my wants.   The reason for life is not to die, but to live for Christ alone. Jesus will be your strength, the arms that will take you home. Jesus, is the rivers that flow with ease, he is the showers that pour in June. Jesus, is the hottest part of our day, the sun so hot at noon. Jesus, is the sounds that are so common, he is the steps you take each day. Jesus, is the moon the stars and the wind, the smiles, and all the time you spend with your heart and mind inclined on the words that where left behind. Today just look inside for the Bible tells no lies, your life will never be the same when you read of the holy name.

41

JESUS IS MY PEN

Jesus

JESUS IS MY PEN

Chapter 5

Jesus Will See You Through

As I look to the distance, I dare not to dream. I have no one to depend on at less that is what it seems. Looking to the future, how will it all work? I have been in prison eight years now that really hurts, I have been placed back into the world without a place to live, how will I get work when I have nothing to give? My mind slowly wonders of what plans God has for me, would he leave me hungry and living in the streets? I truly know the answer, but still I am unaware. As I look into the distance I see my savior standing there, my time will be coming it will be coming very soon. I will leave these prison gates without nothing to lose, my faith holds strong in wisdom to know that God is there. I put my trust in Jesus for he hears my prayers. Looking toward the future, I will make it with God's help. MY job will come from Jesus, he has already ordered me a place to stay as I look toward the future I must keep the faith. I must except everything as a blessing for everything belong to him. Jesus, will see me through until the end of time. What I will do is keep these things in mind.

Transformed

Transformed by the essence, in the beauty of the king.

Growing by his power, the strength only God gives.

I, have blossomed like a flower today I live.

Dressed in the puddles, rooted in love.

I am transformed by the spirit.

Now I am love.

Expand My Territory

Lord, expand my territory lead me back to God's word. I have been freed indeed, as free as the birds. Beyond Venus, beyond Mars, beyond the Moon, beyond the stars. It sounds just like a whisper, something like a chime, it is blowing through the universe it is flowing through my mind. I will give you what you want and everything you need. Just take my hand and come along with me. Across many oceans to the highest hills, your life belongs to me to do my fathers will. Bounty and goodness you will be filled with peace. Praying only in my name, on bending knee. Instructing your life, with a design no one can take. I am using your life only for goodness sake. I have expanded your territory, I have opened the way all you need to do is believe and keep the faith.

Captured Thoughts

With so many words to choose, with this pen and paper I have no time to lose. I have taken so many chances, this is a chance I am willing to take to capture my feelings I can hardly wait. Looking in the distance, a glance at peace of mind with no time to waste for the feeling is so divine. I stumbled upon an adventure, one that would surely feed my dreams. An adventure that gives so much promise, enchanted by what it seems. Captured by a memory that replays itself again. Engulfed by so many people that choose to call me friend. I have landed in my surroundings, in a place I can call home with love and understanding, I will never be alone. Honesty and free spirit-ness surrounds me everywhere, without a care or a worry, just how did I get there? I have passed a lot of troubles disturbing my every thought, I have walked and walked a life time but never giving up. I have been given purpose and planning, one unlike my own. Quality and reassurance that I would not go wrong. Capturing my thoughts how worthy they must be, understanding where I was but now choosing to follow thee. Without regret of any moment, or of any day that has passed by, I am capturing my thoughts without a question why. Growing through the struggles, strengthen through the pain I have captured my thoughts, I stand in Jesus name.

The Light

Thinking on the bliss of light, how the word what I must write. Trusting what is on the page, all the things that is in my head. Wonder somehow fills my mind, I have to write I haven't much time. To complete the sentences in my head, so I write what is said. The purpose how it fills my soul, I will proclaim it so bold. To write the spirit filled phrase, these are Jesus words that I am gave.

JESUS IS MY PEN

Chapter 6

Angel Kiss

On a morning like this, I would not want to miss the beauty of God's mercy looking something like this. The blueness of the skies, the fact that I am alive. Knowing my heart, making me special to God himself. On a morning like this with all the fighting and wars, knowing God gives me purpose and opens doors. Believing God's power, feeling God's strength knowing my name is written on God's list. A time never passes that the saints forget that I am here, with the birds chirping and singing, Jesus is near. On a morning in prison, with so much stress and stride, with so much anger with so much pride. To know I have a friend that helps my every step, believing that God is not finished with me yet. On a morning like this, I awake with a prayer telling the Lord Jesus that I am tired and scared. Thanking God for his mercy, for filling my life with grace allowing me to feel an angel kiss me tenderly on my face. On a morning like this I will never forget, where I have been and just where I have not been yet. My heart is faithful believing in God's word, hearing that Jesus loves me by the chirping of the birds. Feeling God's tenderness, his mercy and his grace, waking me this morning with an angels kiss on my face.

Walking On Water

Walking on water that is what Jesus taught, it allows us to see how far we have been brought. Walking on water, how will we stand? Believing and trusting on Jesus out stretched hand. How do we walk on water, when we stand on dry land? This may be a question, just have faith that Jesus has a plan. This will teach you to be faithful and depend on God's word, spreading the good news to those that have not yet heard. Walking on water, takes an undoubting faith, asking in prayer to see God's faces. You could never recover or go back in time, walking on water will renew your mind. Believing in scripture, as one verse would say always remain prayerful never ceasing to say? Jesus, you are the power, you are my strength the blessing you give no man can send. Jesus, you open doors no man can shut. Jesus, you heal the sick that no man can touch. Walking on water just keep this in mind, Jesus is never late he is always on time.

I Believe In Angels #6

In the middle of winter with on place to call home, God sent me his angel to help me along. Clueless and empty with no one to call friend, Jesus sent me his angel to lend me a hand. Her eyes were a glisten, her heart was a glow. Her arms were wide open, she said "yes I know". Without any questions, no doubt could be found. My angel was present, as real as could be she said "Jesus sent her to me". Her voice was so pleasant, she seemed to know it all she told me "do not fear on Jesus you called, he heard all your prayers. He has freed you indeed, Jesus told me to take you to live with me". My heart skipped a beat, tears filled my eyes my angel was human she wore no disguise. Although some was against me and worked for my demise, I knew in my heart that was all a lie. The truth of my angel, and all the love that she give teaching me honor and the way I should live. All in an instant, as time would stand still. God's miracle appeared, his grace was revealed in the middle of winter with no chance to survive. God sent me an angel to keep me alive.

The Race

We run this race with purpose, we run this race with plan. Don't look to the left or right. Don't be distracted if you can. Follow your faith with dignity, the call for you to grow. God holds your fate and to heaven you will go.

The Beauty Of God

All of God's beauty all covered in rain, every drop
prepared before it hits your window pane.

All of God's beauty all covered in snow, as God himself
said "who could withstand His cold"?

All of God's beauty displayed in the night, the moon and
stars what a wondrous sight.

All of God's beauty as the ray of sun, knowing its place
as the only one.

All of God's beauty set in its place, the trees the meadows
all covered in grace.

Think of the beauties you haven't yet seen, for all of
God's beauty is everything.

JESUS IS MY PEN

Chapter 7

In This Moment In Time

As my mind races back to this moment in time, I realize my sanity was out of time. I wondered thru my life suffering and in pain, I now know that I was completely insane. Living life thinking that I knew it all, I truly thought I was having a ball. Inside myself I was afraid and all alone, I felt left out as if I didn't belong. I tried drugs to help me understand, the usage increased darkness was all I could see with no way out it felt like evil was chasing me. As I wished for a brighter day, I prayed for something to help me find my way. Prison caught me in just a nick of time, my higher power helped to restore my mind. Without a doubt I traveled thru my past, forgiving and being forgiven I was freed at last.

As I race toward this moment in time, I spent several years recovering sitting doing time. Admitting that my life was a mess, I have been restored to sanity I would not have been able to do it without the test. Deciding my life was not my own, given over my life to whom which it rightfully belong. Searching myself to find just what it takes, admitting to God and others all my mistakes. I became entirely ready to remove the evil me, I found humbleness which helped me to be willing to make amends to the persons that I had hurt. I promptly admit the things I had done wrong, I prayed as well as meditation which improved my walk with God. I prayed for the power to carry this out, I believed in Jesus I had no doubt. As I race to reach this moment in time, spiritually I have been awaken by God's power so divine. Through my steps I convey this message to you, Practice these principles in everything that you do. As we reach this moment on time, the things that are against us are all in our mind. Our higher power, God helps us through this race at the finish line we all will see Jesus face to face. As we travel I will hold your hand, because on this race you will need a sober friend.

In Jesus Name

At times my steps are quicken, I am always on the go. Right now I take much caution, it's time to take it slow. My ears are much keener, my heart is filled with joy. I listen for my helper, I listen for Jesus voice. I pay close attention, my sensitivity is high. I am overwhelmed with emotion, I often want to cry. I struggle in understanding, I wait for answers still. I only want to do what is in my holy fathers will. The peace it still surround me, for God remain the same. So every step I take I take in Jesus name.

Meanwhile

Years have passed with so many worries with so many tears, my heart has been broken my body ached with pain. I thought that I would go insane, these years pass to wash me clean, of all the hatred in my heart for any human being. To learn to acknowledge the presence of God, I learned to laugh and love from my heart. To read the bible and witness God's true love, to place my feet beyond and above. These years have passed to help me see, that Jesus loved me so much that he would die for me. Time, so long ago I could not understand how to put my hand in Jesus hand. Meanwhile as I watched the years go by, my worries became fewer and my tears were dried. My heart was mended, my body was healed. My mind was no longer confuse, and on my knees I knelt. To ask my teacher, my helper my friend, to help me guide me and to lend me a hand. To comfort me and to give knowledge that will help me grow, to God's holy word is where I was directed to go. To praise in the sunshine, to praise in the rain. To worship in the valley, to worship beside the streams. To give honor to the most High and His unfailing love, to seek first the kingdom and His power from up above. To see life of plenty, to see life of pain, to see life of abundance and all the blessings it brings. To keep God first in all that you do, to pray for this world as the saints do. To ask for forgiveness and to be aware of the continuous blessings as they appear. To feed the hungry, to cloth the poor, all the things you could not see before. Years and time and much hard work, helped me to understand my true worth. While in the meantime those years that have passed by not only helped me but it has helped you to realize, all my prayers, blessings and all my dreams began in prison but now I am free in deed.

I Can Feel It In The Air

I love the way you love me, I can feel it in the air.

I love the way you love me, I know you truly care.

I love the way you love me, I can hear your sweet sound.

I love the way you love me, I can hear it all around.

I love the way you love me, I live to see your face.

I love the way you love me, the beauty of your grace.

I love the way you love me, the protector of my soul.

I love the way you love me, so big and so bold.

I know that you love me, I can feel it deep within.

I love the way you love me, my dearest and close friend.

I love the way you love me, a love I could never live without.

Your love removes all my fears, and takes away my doubt.

I love the way you love me, no other love could compare.

I love the way you love me, I can feel it in the air.

I Believe In Angels #7

On this day of passing the silence fills its space, knowing that you made it you have finished this earthly race. Feeling your heavenly presents that assures me that you are near. The silence but a whisper that only I can hear. The movement in the distance, soon I will know just how far. The twinkle in the darken skies, you are my brightest star.

The time it pass so quickly, the memories they linger on. My heart is filled with gladness, knowing you made it home. Peace and understanding it fills my heart tonight, knowing that my angel has taken her first flight. This earthly life is over but you lived it oh so well, the treasures you stored in heaven leaves such a lovely trail.

The gifts that I have been given, I replay and replay again. The silence yet a whisper, allows me to hold your hand. Now on this day of passing, realizing that it all was meant to be. To write a pleasant message, or a verse to another song. With each passing moment, I can hear you singing along. At this moment of closing, our story never ends. With each lovely memory you live and live again.

The Oldest Story Ever Told

Throughout the bible it has been told that Jesus was humble yet so bold. He didn't walk like you and I, for he didn't have a sty in his eye. He saw things crystal clear, we believe things that we see not what we hear. Anytime that Jesus walked thru the door, no lies, no shame nothing impure. JESUS always told the truth his life endure. He knew just how to make you feel, for he done only what his father willed. Jesus prayed, he healed, and he set souls free he did all these things for you and me. Jesus taught, he preached, he praised the Lord, the light is what is called his word. Jesus spoke to sinners like you and I, so many learned to be thankful and acknowledge, and so aware that Jesus truly cared. For all along he knew that in the end he would die, to take our sins away. On that day of crucifixion he never spoke he only listened, to lies, to hatred to all that was wrong. Jesus knew he was on his way home, the thief that hung so very close he did not brag he did not boast. He only asked if he could go, as if he knew that home

JESUS IS MY PEN

was on the thrown. The soldiers stood still, as my Jesus died as their eyes looked on darken skies. I only could imagine what feeling swept, I know that some even wept. I ask the Lord Jesus for faith here today, to keep me close till my dying day. I am one of them that loves to walk and talk with him. Just like the sinner that hung so close, I only brag, I only boast on all the love that Jesus has given me. To know he heals and allows me to see, the beautiful light his Holy Word. I love to hear what he has told to every race and creed that if we just believe in him that he will return again. Jesus is coming to take us with him, where there is no crying, no pain, not a spot of sin that we all would be next to kin. Jesus proclaims, that we would sing and dance and be filled with joy. Jesus says there will be death no more, I believe that the time is near, just have the faith and have no fear. Jesus says, he will come like the twinkling of the eye, now it is time to learn to die.

Words That Changed History

Our thoughts change the way we think and the way we are taught changes the way we live. The words were delivered to the world, those who wanted to hear them or not, those words were the seeds they got. Those words came loud and clear, those words brought nations near. Those words were not just black and white, those words changed wrong to right. Those words made flags fly high, those words made countries cry. Those words helped freedom ring, those words caused people to sing. Those words that were spoken that day, we all heard a man say.

Free at last, thank

God almighty I am free at last.

Image

Take a look in the mirror and what do you see? A woman, a man, a little baby. Standing in the midst of the things unseen. When you look in the mirror, a reflection appears. Open your heart, open your ears. Open your eyes and discover the sights. God is inside us, with all of his might. The creator of heaven, the maker of earth. The master of life, the giver of birth. The hands that will hold you, so gentle and strong. The hands that this world rest upon. Now, look in the mirror and without a doubt, the image of God shows inside and out.

Conclusion

Come to Jesus Christ today

JESUS IS MY PEN

About The Author

Lily Thompson was born in the early 1960's in Mount Clemans Michigan to a single mother. She was named after her grandmother the late Lily Thomas. As times grew harder for her mother to care for she and her siblings, they were removed from her mother's home and placed in foster care for several years. In 1972 Lily was adopted to the wonderful Mr.& Mrs. William H. Thompson Sr. who changed her name to Lily Thompson. In 1986 she joined the U.S. Army. Completing a full term of eight years. The armed forces took her many places. She has even traveled abroad to places such as France, as well as Germany. She attended Robert Morris College in

Chicago Ill, earning an associated degree in applied science. She has also earned an understudy certificate through Oakland City University in Business Tech. In 2012 she became a member of Toastmaster's International earning her silver certificate in the advance public speaking series. Lily now lives in Madison, IN.

JESUS IS MY PEN

JESUS IS MY PEN

www.ingramcontent.com/pod-product-compliance
Lightning Source LLC
Chambersburg PA
CBHW060423050426
42449CB00009B/2104